# The Complete Lyric Poetry

# Andrew Marvell

# CONTENTS

# INTRODUCTION

Andrew Marvell (1621 – 1678) remains an enigma for two key reasons: we lack key knowledge about aspects of his life, and his poetry seems to contain many inconsistencies and ambivalences. Apart from "An Horatian Ode…" none of the poems in this book were published while he lived and, while there is an assumption about when they were written, we do not know for certain.

Marvell was brought up in Hull, where his father was a minister in the local church, and he went to Cambridge at the age of twelve, being awarded his BA in 1639. In 1641 his father died by drowning in the Humber estuary and Marvell seems to have abandoned his studies. It is widely assumed that he spent the years of the Civil War travelling in Europe, but there is no solid evidence for this, and it would be strange had he done so, because in later life he was associated very firmly with the parliamentary cause. Certainly by 1649 he was living in Yorkshire and acting as tutor to Maria Fairfax, the daughter of Sir Thomas Fairfax, who had been Commander in Chief of the Parliamentary Army which had so decisively beaten the King. There is strong internal evidence that most of Marvell's lyric poems were written during this time – obviously "Upon Appleton House" which is about Fairfax's country estate and in which Maria Fairfax appears. Marvell went on to act as a tutor to a ward of Oliver Cromwell and in 1657 was appointed Latin Secretary to Milton in Cromwell's government. Latin was the lingua franca of European diplomacy. In 1660, when the monarchy was restored, Marvell was elected MP for Hull, a constituency he continued to represent until his sudden death in 1678. This period of his life is one we know quite a lot about. As an MP, Marvell was a public figure and he tended to defend the interests of freedom, free speech and religious toleration against the less tolerant and more royalist tendency in Parliament. He wrote a great deal during this period – verse satires and prose pamphlets and books which attacked and lampooned his political opponents.

Marvell's poems are full of oppositions and dichotomies – seen at their most obvious in the Dialogue poems where he presents two opposed and intransigent voices. Some of his poems are the finest in the pastoral tradition – but there is a constant tension between the peace, tranquility and isolation of the countryside, and the urge to be active or poems where that peace and tranquility are destroyed by some external force: one thinks of the Mower poems where the Mower's innocent life is completely disrupted by the arrival of Juliana or "The Nymph Complaining for the Death of her Fawn". Even in "The Horatian Ode" we are told that Cromwell had to leave his "private gardens" to pursue his "active star" and take part in the Civil War. But activity or busy-ness always takes a terrible toll on the participants in Marvell's poetry. Leaving the garden and the sanctuary of nature tends to wound and damage the individual. Nowhere is this more apparent than in "Upon Appleton House" in which Marvell starts at Lord Fairfax's house, but is driven away from the garden, then into the meadows and finally finds sanctuary and complete peace only in the heart of the wood. What has driven him away from civilization? The Civil War and memories of it: stanzas XLI - XLIII of this poem are a plangent lament for what the war has done to England: destroyed its innocence. And those two opposing ideas – innocence and experience – apply to so many poems of Marvell: innocence associated with nature, youth, passivity, the word 'green', simplicity, a relaxed idleness and a yearning for quiet sanctuary whether in this world ("The Garden"), the next ("On a Drop of Dew" or another one altogether ("Bermudas"); experience with war, women, adulthood, politics and a striving for success and fulfillment whether in love or war.

## A Dialogue between the Resolved Soul and Created Pleasure

Courage, my soul! now learn to wield

The weight of thine immortal shield;

Close on thy head thy helmet bright;

Balance thy sword against the fight;

See where an army, strong as fair,

With silken banners spreads the air!

Now, if thou be'st that thing divine,

In this day's combat let it shine,

And show that Nature wants an art

To conquer one resolvèd heart.

### Pleasure

Welcome the creation's guest,

Lord of earth, and Heaven's heir!

Lay aside that warlike crest,

And of Nature's banquet share;

Where the souls of fruits and flowers

Stand prepared to heighten yours.

### Soul

I sup above, and cannot stay,

To bait so long upon the way.

**Pleasure**

On these downy pillows lie,

Whose soft plumes will thither fly:

On these roses, strowed so plain

Lest one leaf thy side should strain.

**Soul**

My gentler rest is on a thought,

Conscious of doing what I ought.

**Pleasure**

If thou be'st with perfumes pleased,

Such as oft the gods appeased,

Thou in fragrant clouds shalt show,

Like another god below.

**Soul**

A soul that knows not to presume,

Is Heaven's, and its own, perfume.

**Pleasure**

Everything does seem to vie

Which should first attract thine eye:

But since none deserves that grace,

In this crystal view thy face.

**Soul**

When the Creator's skill is prized,

The rest is all but earth disguised.


**Pleasure**

Hark how music then prepares

For thy stay these charming airs,

Which the posting winds recall,

And suspend the river's fall.


**Soul**

Had I but any time to lose,

On this I would it all dispose.

Cease, tempter! None can chain a mind,

Whom this sweet cordage cannot bind.


**Chorus**

Earth cannot show so brave a sight,

  As when a single soul does fence

  The batteries of alluring sense,

And Heaven views it with delight.

  Then persevere;  for still new charges sound,

    And if thou overcom'st thou shalt be crowned.


**Pleasure**

All that's costly, fair, and sweet,

Which scatteringly doth shine,

Shall within one beauty meet,

   And she be only thine.

**Soul**

 If things of sight such heavens be,

What heavens are those we cannot see?

**Pleasure**

 Wheresoe'er thy foot shall go

   The minted gold shall lie,

Till thou purchase all below,

   And want new worlds to buy.

**Soul**

 We'rt not for price who'd value gold?

And that's worth naught that can be sold.

**Pleasure**

 Wilt thou all the glory have

   That war or peace commend?

Half the world shall be thy slave,

   The other half thy friend.

**Soul**

 What friend, if to my self untrue?

What slaves, unless I captive you?

**Pleasure**

Thou shalt know each hidden cause,
  And see the future time;
Try what depth the centre draws,
  And then to Heaven climb.

**Soul**

None thither mounts by the degree
Of knowledge, but humility.

**Chorus**

Triumph, triumph, victorious soul!
  The world has not one pleasure more:
The rest does lie beyond the pole,
  And is thine everlasting store.

## Eyes and Tears

How wisely Nature did decree,
With the same Eyes to weep and see!
That, having view'd the object vain,
They might be ready to complain.

And since the Self-deluding Sight,
In a false Angle takes each hight;
These Tears which better measure all,
Like wat'ry Lines and Plummets fall.

Two Tears, which Sorrow long did weigh
Within the Scales of either Eye,
And then paid out in equal Poise,
Are the true price of all my Joyes.

What in the World most fair appears,
Yea even Laughter, turns to Tears:
And all the Jewels which we prize,
Melt in these Pendants of the Eyes.

I have through every Garden been,
Amongst the Red, the White, the Green;
And yet, from all the flow'rs I saw,
No Hony, but these Tears could draw.

So the all-seeing Sun each day

Distills the World with Chymick Ray;

But finds the Essence only Showers,

Which straight in pity back he powers.


Yet happy they whom Grief doth bless,

That weep the more, and see the less:

And, to preserve their Sight more true,

Bath still their Eyes in their own Dew.


So Magdalen, in Tears more wise

Dissolv'd those captivating Eyes,

Whose liquid Chains could flowing meet

To fetter her Redeemer's feet.


Not full sailes hasting loaden home,

Nor the chast Ladies pregnant Womb,

Nor Cynthia Teeming show's so fair,

As two Eyes swoln with weeping are.


The sparkling Glance that shoots Desire,

Drench'd in these Waves, does lose it fire.

Yea oft the Thund'rer pitty takes

And here the hissing Lightning slakes.

The Incense was to Heaven dear,

Not as a Perfume, but a Tear.

And Stars shew lovely in the Night,

But as they seem the Tears of Light.


Ope then mine Eyes your double Sluice,

And practise so your noblest Use.

For others too can see, or sleep;

But only humane Eyes can weep.


Now like two Clouds dissolving, drop,

And at each Tear in distance stop:

Now like two Fountains trickle down:

Now like two floods o'return and drown.


Thus let your Streams o'reflow your Springs,

Till Eyes and Tears be the same things:

And each the other's difference bears;

These weeping Eyes, those seeing Tears.

## On a Drop of Dew

See how the orient dew

Shed from the bosom of the Morn

Into the blowing roses,

Yet careless of its mansion new,

For the clear region where 'twas born,

Round in its self incloses:

And in its little globe's extent

Frames, as it can, its native element.

How it the purple flow'r does slight,

Scarce touching where it lyes,

But gazing back upon the skies,

Shines with a mournful light,

Like its own tear,

Because so long divided from the sphere.

Restless it roules, and unsecure,

Trembling, lest it grow impure;

Till the warm sun pitty its pain

And to the skies exhale it back again.

So the soul, that drop, that ray,

Of the clear fountain of eternal day,

(Could it within the humane flow'r be seen)

Rememb'ring still its former height,

Shuns the sweat leaves and blossoms green,

And, recollecting its own light,

Does in its pure and circling thoughts express

The greater heaven in an heaven less.

In how coy a figure wound,

Every way it turns away;

(So the world-excluding round)

Yet receiving in the day.

Dark beneath, but bright above,

Here disdaining, there in love.

How loose and easie hence to go;

How girt and ready to ascend;

Moving but on a point below,

It all about does upwards bend.

Such did the manna's sacred dew destil,

White and intire, though congeal'd and chill;

Congeal'd on Earth; but does, dissolving, run

Into the glories of th' almighty sun.

# Bermudas

Where the remote Bermudas ride

In the ocean's bosom unespied,

From a small boat that row'd along

The listening woods received this song:


'What should we do but sing His praise

That led us through the watery maze

Unto an isle so long unknown,

And yet far kinder than our own?

Where He the huge sea-monsters wracks,

That lift the deep upon their backs,

He lands us on a grassy stage,

Safe from the storms' and prelates' rage:

He gave us this eternal Spring

Which here enamels everything,

And sends the fowls to us in care

On daily visits through the air:

He hangs in shades the orange bright

Like golden lamps in a green night,

And does in the pomegranates close

Jewels more rich than Ormus shows:

He makes the figs our mouths to meet

And throws the melons at our feet;

But apples plants of such a price,

No tree could ever bear them twice.

With cedars chosen by His hand

From Lebanon He stores the land;

And makes the hollow seas that roar

Proclaim the ambergris on shore.

He cast (of which we rather boast)

The Gospel's pearl upon our coast;

And in these rocks for us did frame

A temple where to sound His name.

O, let our voice His praise exalt

Till it arrive at Heaven's vault,

Which thence (perhaps) rebounding may

Echo beyond the Mexique bay!'


Thus sung they in the English boat

A holy and a cheerful note:

And all the way, to guide their chime,

With falling oars they kept the time.

## The Coronet

When for the thorns with which I long, too long,
With many a piercing wound,
My Saviour's head have crowned,
I seek with garlands to redress that wrong,
Through every garden, every mead,
I gather flowers (my fruits are only flowers),
Dismantling all the fragrant towers
That once adorned my shepherdess's head:
And now, when I have summed up all my store,
Thinking (so I my self deceive)
So rich a chaplet thence to weave
As never yet the King of Glory wore,
Alas ! I find the Serpent old,
That, twining in his speckled breast,
About the flowers disguised, does fold
With wreaths of fame and interest.
Ah, foolish man, that wouldst debase with them,
And mortal glory, Heaven's diadem !
But thou who only couldst the Serpent tame,
Either his slippery knots at once untie,
And disentangle all his winding snare,
Or shatter too with him my curious frame,
And let these wither—so that he may die—
Though set with skill, and chosen out with care;
That they, while thou on both their spoils dost tread,
May crown Thy feet, that could not crown Thy head.

## Clorinda and Damon

Clorinda:

Damon come drive thy flocks this way.

Damon:

No : 'tis too late they went astray.

C:

I have a grassy Scutcheon spy'd,

Where Flora blazons all her pride.

The grass I aim to feast thy Sheep:

The Flow'rs I for thy Temples keep.

D:

Grass withers; and the Flow'rs too fade.

C:

Seize the short Joyes then, ere they vade.

Seest thou that unfrequented Cave?

D:

That den?

C:

Loves Shrine.

D:

But Virtue's Grave.

C:

In whose cool bosome we may lye

Safe from the Sun.

D:

Not Heaven's Eye.

C:

Near this, a Fountaines liquid Bell

Tinkles within the concave Shell.

D:

Might a Soul bath there and be clean,

Or slake its Drought?

C:

What is 't you mean?

D:

These once had been enticing things,

Clorinda, Pastures, Caves, and Springs.

C:

And what late change?

D:

The other day

Pan met me.

C:

What did great Pan say?

D:

Words that transcend poor Shepherds skill,

But he ere since my Songs does fill:

And his Name swells my slender Oate.

C:

Sweet must Pan sound in Damon's Note.

D:

Clorinda's voice might make it sweet.

C:

Who would not in Pan's Praises meet?

**Chorus**

Of Pan the flowry pastures sing,

Caves eccho and the Fountains ring.

Sing then while he doth us inspire;

For all the world is our Pan's Quire.

# Two Songs at the Marriage of The Lord Fauconberg and The Lady Mary Cromwell

## Chorus

Th' Astrologers own Eyes are set,

And even Wolves the Sheep forget;

Only this Shepherd, late and soon,

Upon this Hill outwakes the Moon.

Heark how he sings, with sad delight,

Thorough the clear and silent Night.

## Endymion

Cynthia, O Cynthia, turn thine Ear,

nor scorn Endymion's plaints to hear.

As we our Flocks, so you command

The fleecy Clouds with silver wand.

## Cynthia

If thou a Mortal, rather sleep;

Or if a Shepherd, watch thy Sheep.

## Endmymion

The Shepherd, since he saw thine Eyes,

And Sheep are both thy Sacrifice.

Nor merits he a Mortal's name,

That burns with an immortal Flame.

**Cynthia**

I have enough for me to do,

Ruling the Waves that Ebb and Flow.


**Endymion**

Since thou disdain'st not then to share

On Sublunary things thy Care;

Rather restrain these double Seas,

Mine Eyes uncessant deluges.


**Cynthia**

My wakeful Lamp all night must move,

Securing their Repose above.


**Endymion**

If therefore thy resplendent Ray

Can make a Night more bright then Day;

Shine thorough this obscurer Brest,

With shades of deep Despair opprest.


**Chorus**

Courage, Endymion, boldly Woo,

Anchises was a Shepheard too:

Yet is her younger Sister laid

Sporting with him in Ida's shade:

And Cynthia, though the strongest,

Seeks but the honour to have held out longest.

**Endymion**

Here unto Latmos Top I climbe:

How far below thine Orbe sublime?

O why, as well as Eyes to see,

Have I not Armes that reach to thee?

**Cynthia**

'Tis needless then that I refuse,

Would you but your own Reason use.

**Endymion**

Though I so high may not pretend,

It is the same so you descend.

**Cynthia**

These Stars would say I do them wrong,

Rivals each one for thee too strong.

**Endymion**

The Stars are fix'd unto their Sphere,

And cannot, though they would, come near.

Less Loves set of each other's praise,

While Stars Eclypse by mixing Rayes.

**Cynthia**

That Cave is dark.

**Endymion**

Then none can spy:

Or shine Thou there and 'tis the Sky.

**Chorus**

Joy to Endymion,

For he has Cynthia's favour won.

And Jove himself approves

With his serenest influence their Loves.

For he did never love to pair

His Progeny above the Air;

But to be honest, valiant, wise,

Makes Mortals matches fit for Deityes.

### Second Song

**Hobbinol**

Phillis, Tomalin, away:

Never such a merry day.

For the Northern Shepheard's Son

Has Menalca's daughter won.

**Phillis**

Stay till I some flow'rs ha'ty'd

In a Garland for the Bride.


**Tomalin**

If Thou would'st a Garland bring,

Philiis you may wait the Spring:

They ha' chosen such an hour

When She is the only flow'r.


**Phillis**

Let's not then at least be seen

Without each a Sprig of Green.


**Hobbinol**

Fear not; at Menalca's Hall

There is Bayes enough for all.

He when Young as we did graze,

But when Old he planted Bayes.


**Tomalin**

Here She comes; but with a Look

Far more catching then my Hook.

'Twas those Eyes, I now dare swear,

Led our Lambs we knew not where.

### Hobbinol

Not our Lambs own Fleeces are

Curl'd so lovely as her Hair:

Nor our Sheep new Wash'd can be

Half so white or sweet as She.

### Phillis

He so looks as fit to keep

Somewhat else then silly Sheep.

### Hobbinol

Come, lets in some Carol new

Pay to Love and Them their due.

### All

Joy to that happy Pair,

Whose Hopes united banish our Despair.

What Shepheard could for Love pretend,

Whil'st all the Nymphs on Damon's choice attend?

What Shepherdess could hope to wed

Before Marina's turn were sped?

Now lesser Beauties may take place,

And meaner Virtues come in play;

While they,

Looking from high,

Shall grace

Our Flocks and us with a propitious Eye.

But what is most, the gentle Swain

No more shall need of Love complain;

But Virtue shall be Beauties hire,

And those be equal that have equal Fire.

Or who despair, now Damon does enjoy?

Marina yields. Who dares be coy?

Joy to that happy Pair,

Whose Hopes united banish our Despair.

## A Dialogue between the Soul and Body

Soul:
O, who shall from this dungeon raise
A soul enslaved so many ways?
With bolts of bones, that fettered stands
In feet, and manacled in hands;
Here blinded with an eye, and there
Deaf with the drumming of an ear;
A soul hung up, as 'twere, in chains
Of nerves, and arteries, and veins;
Tortured, besides each other part,
In a vain head, and double heart?

Body:
O, who shall me deliver whole,
From bonds of this tyrannic soul?
Which, stretched upright, impales me so
That mine own precipice I go;
And warms and moves this needless frame,
(A fever could but do the same),
And, wanting where its spite to try,
Has made me live to let me die
A body that could never rest,
Since this ill spirit it possessed.

Soul:
What magic could me thus confine
Within another's grief to pine?
Where, whatsoever it complain,
I feel, that cannot feel, the pain;
And all my care itself employs,
That to preserve which me destroys;
Constrained not only to endure
Diseases, but, what's worse, the cure;
And, ready oft the port to gain,
Am shipwrecked into health again.

Body:
But Physic yet could never reach
The maladies thou me dost teach;
Whom first the cramp of hope does tear,
And then the palsy shakes of fear;
The pestilence of love does heat,
Or hatred's hidden ulcer eat;
Joy's cheerful madness does perplex,
Or sorrow's other madness vex;
Which knowledge forces me to know,
And memory will not forego;
What but a soul could have the wit
To build me up for sin so fit?
So architects do square and hew
Green trees that in the forest grew.

## The Nymph Complaining for the
## Death of her Fawn

The wanton troopers riding by
Have shot my fawn, and it will die.
Ungentle men! they cannot thrive
Who killed thee. Thou ne'er didst alive
Them any harm, alas! nor could
Thy death yet do them any good.
I'm sure I never wished them ill ;
Nor do I for all this, nor will :
But, if my simple prayers may yet
Prevail with Heaven to forget
Thy murder, I will join my tears,
Rather than fail.   But, O my fears!
It cannot die so. Heaven's king
Keeps register of everything,
And nothing may we use in vain;
Even beasts must be with justice slain,
Else men are made their deodands.
Though they should wash their guilty hands
In this warm life-blood which doth part
From thine, and wound me to the heart,
Yet could they not be clean; their stain
Is dyed in such a purple grain.
There is not such another in

The world, to offer for their sin.

Unconstant SYLVIO, when yet

I had not found him counterfeit,

One morning (I remember well),

Tied in this silver chain and bell,

Gave it to me: nay, and I know

What he said then, I'm sure I do:

Said he, "Look how your huntsman here

Hath taught a fawn to hunt his deer."

But SYLVIO soon had me beguiled;

This waxèd tame, while he grew wild,

And quite regardless of my smart,

Left me his fawn, but took his heart.

Thenceforth I set myself to play

My solitary time away,

With this; and very well content,

Could so mine idle life have spent;

For it was full of sport, and light

Of foot and heart, and did invite

Me to its game: it seemed to bless

Itself in me; how could I less

Than love it? O, I cannot be

Unkind to a beast that loveth me.

Had it lived long, I do not know

Whether it too might have done so

As SYLVIO did; his gifts might be

Perhaps as false, or more, than he;

But I am sure, for aught that I

Could in so short a time espy,

Thy love was far more better then

The love of false and cruel men.

With sweetest milk and sugar first

I it at mine own fingers nursed;

And as it grew, so every day

It waxed more white and sweet than they.

It had so sweet a breath! And oft

I blushed to see its foot more soft

And white, shall I say than my hand?

Nay, any lady's of the land.

It is a wondrous thing how fleet

'Twas on those little silver feet;

With what a pretty skipping grace

It oft would challenge me the race;

And, when't had left me far away,

'Twould stay, and run again, and stay;

For it was nimbler much than hinds,

And trod as if on the four winds.

I have a garden of my own,

But so with roses overgrown,

And lilies, that you would it guess

To be a little wilderness;

And all the spring-time of the year

It only lovèd to be there.

Among the beds of lilies I

Have sought it oft, where it should lie,

Yet could not, till itself would rise,

Find it, although before mine eyes;

For, in the flaxen lilies' shade,

It like a bank of lilies laid.

Upon the roses it would feed,

Until its lips e'en seem to bleed

And then to me 'twould boldly trip,

And print those roses on my lip.

But all its chief delight was still

On roses thus itself to fill,

And its pure virgin limbs to fold

In whitest sheets of lilies cold:

Had it lived long, it would have been

Lilies without, roses within.

O help! O help! I see it faint

And die as calmly as a saint!

See how it weeps! the tears do come

Sad, slowly, dropping like a gum.

So weeps the wounded balsam; so

The holy frankincense doth flow;

The brotherless Heliades

Melt in such amber tears as these.

I in a golden vial will

Keep these two crystal tears, and fill

It till it do o'erflow with mine,

Then place it in DIANA'Sshrine.

Now my sweet fawn is vanished to

Whither the swans and turtles go;

In fair Elysium to endure,

With milk-like lambs, and ermines pure.

O do not run too fast: for I

Will but bespeak thy grave, and die.

First, my unhappy statue shall

Be cut in marble; and withal

Let it be weeping too; but there

The engraver sure his art may spare;

For I so truly thee bemoan,

That I shall weep, though I be stone,

Until my tears, still dropping, wear

My breast, themselves engraving there;

There at my feet shalt thou be laid,

Of purest alabaster made;

For I would have thine image be

White as I can, though not as thee.

## Young Love

Come little infant, love me now,
    While thine unsuspected years
Clear thine agèd father's brow
    From cold jealousy and fears.


Pretty surely 'twere to see
    By young Love old Time beguiled,
While our sportings are as free
    As the nurse's with the child.


Common beauties stay fifteen;
    Such as yours should swifter move,
Whose fair blossoms are too green
    Yet for lust, but not for love.


Love as much the snowy lamb,
    Or the wanton kid, does prize,
As the lusty bull or ram,
    For his morning sacrifice.

Now then love me: Time may take
   Thee before thy time away;
Of this need we'll virtue make,
   And learn love before we may.


So we win of doubtful Fate,
   And, if good she to us meant,
We that good shall antedate,
   Or, if ill, that ill prevent.


Thus as kingdoms, frustrating
   Other titles to their crown,
In the cradle crown their king,
   So all foreign claims to drown;


So to make all rivals vain,
   Now I crown thee with my love:
Crown me with thy love again,
   And we both shall monarchs prove.

## To his Coy Mistress

Had we but world enough, and time,
This coyness, lady, were no crime.
We would sit down and think which way
To walk, and pass our long love's day;
Thou by the Indian Ganges' side
Shouldst rubies find; I by the tide
Of Humber would complain. I would
Love you ten years before the Flood;
And you should, if you please, refuse
Till the conversion of the Jews.
My vegetable love should grow
Vaster than empires, and more slow.
An hundred years should go to praise
Thine eyes, and on thy forehead gaze;
Two hundred to adore each breast,
But thirty thousand to the rest;
An age at least to every part,
And the last age should show your heart.
For, lady, you deserve this state,
Nor would I love at lower rate.

But at my back I always hear
Time's winged chariot hurrying near;
And yonder all before us lie

Deserts of vast eternity.

Thy beauty shall no more be found,

Nor, in thy marble vault, shall sound

My echoing song; then worms shall try

That long preserv'd virginity,

And your quaint honour turn to dust,

And into ashes all my lust.

The grave's a fine and private place,

But none I think do there embrace.


Now therefore, while the youthful hue

Sits on thy skin like morning dew,

And while thy willing soul transpires

At every pore with instant fires,

Now let us sport us while we may;

And now, like am'rous birds of prey,

Rather at once our time devour,

Than languish in his slow-chapp'd power.

Let us roll all our strength, and all

Our sweetness, up into one ball;

And tear our pleasures with rough strife

Thorough the iron gates of life.

Thus, though we cannot make our sun

Stand still, yet we will make him run.

## The Unfortunate Lover

Alas! how pleasant are their days,
With whom the infant love yet plays!
Sorted by pairs, they still are seen
By fountains cool and shadows green;
But soon these flames do lose their light,
Like meteors of a summer's night;
Nor can they to that region climb,
To make impression upon Time.

   'Twas in a shipwreck, when the seas
Ruled, and the winds did what they please,
That my poor lover floating lay,
And, ere brought forth, was cast away;
Till at the last the master wave
Upon the rock his mother drave,
And there she split against the stone,
In a Cæsarian section.

The sea him lent these bitter tears,
Which at his eyes he always bears,
And from the winds the sighs he bore,
Which through his surging breast do roar;
No day he saw but that which breaks
Through frighted clouds in forkèd streaks,
While round the rattling thunder hurled,
As at the funeral of the world.

While Nature to his birth presents
This masque of quarrelling elements,
A numerous fleet of cormorants black,
That sailed insulting o'er the wrack,
Received into their cruel care,
The unfortunate and abject heir;
Guardians most fit to entertain
The orphan of the hurricane.

They fed him up with hopes and air,

Which soon digested to despair,
And as one cormorant fed him, still
Another on his heart did bill;
Thus, while they famish him and feast,
He both consumèd, and increased,
And languishèd with doubtful breath,
The amphibium of life and death.

And now, when angry Heaven would
Behold a spectacle of blood,
Fortune and he are called to play
At sharp before it all the day,
And tyrant Love his breast does ply
With all his winged artillery,
Whilst he, betwixt the flames and waves,
Like Ajax, the mad tempest braves.

See how he nak'd and fierce does stand,
Cuffing the thunder with one hand,
While with the other he does lock,
And grapple, with the stubborn rock;
From which he with each wave rebounds,
Torn into flames, and ragg'd with wounds;
And all he says, a lover drest
In his own blood does relish best.

This is the only banneret
That ever Love created yet;
Who, though by the malignant stars,
Forcèd to live in storms and wars,
Yet dying, leaves a perfume here,
And music within every ear;
And he in story only rules,
In a field sable, a lover gules.

## The Gallery

Chlora, come view my soul, and tell
Whether I have contrived it well:
Now all its several lodgings lie,
Composed into one gallery,
And the great arras-hangings, made
Of various facings, by are laid,
That, for all furniture, you'll find
Only your picture in my mind.

Here thou art painted in the dress
Of an inhuman murderess;
Examining upon our hearts,
(Thy fertile shop of cruel arts,)
Engines more keen than ever yet
Adornèd tryant's cabinet,
Of which the most tormenting are,
Black eyes, red lips, and curlèd hair.

But, on the other side, thou'rt drawn,
Like to AURORA in the dawn;
When in the east she slumbering lies,
And stretches out her milky thighs,
While all the morning quire does sing,
And manna falls and roses spring,

And, at thy feet, the wooing doves
Sit perfecting their harmless loves.

Like an enchantress here thou show'st,
Vexing thy restless lover's ghost;
And, by a light obscure, dost rave
Over his entrails, in the cave,
Divining thence, with horrid care,
How long thou shalt continue fair;
And (when informed) them throw'st away
To be the greedy vulture's prey.

But, against that, thou sitt'st afloat,
Like VENUS in her pearly boat;
The halcyons, calming all that's nigh,
Betwixt the air and water fly;
Or, if some rolling wave appears,
A mass of ambergris it bears,
Nor blows more wind than what may well
Convoy the perfume to the smell.

These pictures, and a thousand more,
Of thee, my gallery doth store,
In all the forms thou canst invent,
Either to please me, or torment;
For thou alone, to people me,

Art grown a numerous colony,

And a collection choicer far

Than or Whitehall's, or Mantua's were.


But of these pictures, and the rest,

That at the entrance likes me best,

Where the same posture and the look

Remains with which I first was took;

A tender shepherdess, whose hair

Hangs loosely playing in the air,

Transplanting flowers from the green hill,

To crown her head and bosom fill.

## The Fair Singer

To make a final conquest of all me,
Love did compose so sweet an enemy,
In whom both beauties to my death agree,
Joining themselves in fatal harmony,
That, while she with her eyes my heart does bind,
She with her voice might captivate my mind.


I could have fled from one but singly fair;
My disentangled soul itself might save,
Breaking the curlèd trammels of her hair;
But how should I avoid to be her slave,
When subtle art invisibly can wreathe
My fetters of the very air I breathe?


It had been easy fighting in some plain,
Where victory might hang in equal choice,
But all resistance against her is vain,
Who has the advantage both of eyes and voice;
And all my forces needs must be undone,
She having gainèd both the wind and sun.

## Mourning

You, that decipher out the Fate
Of humane Off-springs from the Skies,
What mean these Infants which of late
Spring from the Starrs of *Chlora*'s Eyes?

Her Eyes confus'd, and doubled ore,
With Tears suspended ere they flow;
Seem bending upwards, to restore
To Heaven, whence it came, their Woe:

When, molding off the watry Sphears,
Slow drops unty themselves away;
As if she, with those precious Tears,
Would strow the ground where *Strephon* lay.

Yet some affirm, pretending Art,
Her Eyes have so her Bosome drown'd,
Only to soften near her Heart
A place to fix another Wound.

And, while vain Pomp does her restrain
Within her solitary Bowr,
She courts her self in am'rous Rain;

Her self both *Danae* and the Showr.

Nay others, bolder, hence esteem
Joy now so much her Master grown,
That whatsoever does but seem
Like Grief, is from her Windows thrown.

Nor that she payes, while she survives,
To her dead Love this Tribute due;
But casts abroad these Donatives,
At the installing of a new.

How wide they dream! The *Indian* Slaves
That sink for Pearl through Seas profound,
Would find her Tears yet deeper Waves
And not of one the bottom sound.

I yet my silent Judgment keep,
Disputing not what they believe:
But sure as oft as Women weep,
It is to be suppos'd they grieve.

## Daphnis and Chloe

*Daphnis* must from *Chloe* part:
Now is come the dismal Hour
That must all his Hopes devour,
All his Labour, all his Art.

Nature, her own Sexes foe,
Long had taught her to be coy:
But she neither knew t' enjoy,
Nor yet let her Lover go.

But, with this sad News surpriz'd,
Soon she let that Niceness fall;
And would gladly yield to all,
So it had his stay compriz'd.

Nature so her self does use
To lay by her wonted State,
Left the World should separate;
Sudden Parting closer glews.

He, well read in all the wayes
By which men their Siege maintain,
Knew not that the Fort to gain

Better 'twas the siege to raise.

But he came so full possest
With the Grief of Parting thence,
That he had not so much Sence
As to see he might be blest.

Till Love in her Language breath'd
Words she never spake before;
But than Legacies no more
To a dying Man bequeath'd.

For, Alas, the time was spent,
Now the latest minut's run
When poor *Daphnis* is undone,
Between Joy and Sorrow rent.

At that *Why*, that *Stay my Dear*,
His disorder'd Locks he tare;
And with rouling Eyes did glare,
And his cruel Fate forswear.

As the Soul of one scarce dead,
With the shrieks of Friends aghast,
Looks distracted back in hast,
And then streight again is fled.

So did wretched *Daphnis* look,
Frighting her he loved most.
At the last, this Lovers Ghost
Thus his Leave resolved took.

Are my Hell and Heaven Joyn'd
More to torture him that dies?
Could departure not suffice,
But that you must then grow kind?

Ah my *Chloe* how have I
Such a wretched minute found,
When thy Favours should me wound
More than all thy Cruelty?

So to the condemned Wight
The delicious Cup we fill;
And allow him all he will,
For his last and short Delight.

But I will not now begin
Such a Debt unto my Foe;
Nor to my Departure owe
What my Presence could not win.

Absence is too much alone:
Better 'tis to go in peace,
Than my Losses to increase
By a late Fruition.

Why should I enrich my Fate?
'Tis a Vanity to wear,
For my Executioner,
Jewels of so high a rate.

Rather I away will pine
In a manly stubborness
Than be fatted up express
For the *Canibal* to dine.

Whilst this grief does thee disarm,
All th' Enjoyment of our Love
But the ravishment would prove
Of a Body dead while warm.

And I parting should appear
Like the Gourmand *Hebrew* dead,
While with Quailes and *Manna* fed,
He does through the Desert err;

Or the Witch that midnight wakes

For the Fern, whose magick Weed

In one minute casts the Seed,

And invisible him makes.


Gentler times for Love are ment:

Who for parting pleasure strain

Gather Roses in the rain,

Wet themselves and spoil their Sent.


Farewel therefore all the fruit

Which I could from Love receive:

Joy will not with Sorrow weave,

Nor will I this Grief pollute.


Fate I come, as dark, as sad,

As thy Malice could desire;

Yet bring with me all the Fire

That Love in his Torches had.


At these words away he broke;

As who long has praying ly'n,

To his Heads-man makes the Sign,

And receives the parting stroke.

But hence Virgins all beware.
Last night he with *Phlogis* slept;
This night for *Dorinda* kept;
And but rid to take the Air.

Yet he does himself excuse;
Nor indeed without a Cause.
For, according to the Lawes,
Why did *Chloe* once refuse?

## The Definition of Love

My Love is of a birth as rare
    As 'tis, for object, strange and high;
It was begotten by Despair,
    Upon Impossibility.

Magnanimous Despair alone
    Could show me so divine a thing,
Where feeble hope could ne'er have flown,
    But vainly flapped its tinsel wing.

And yet I quickly might arrive
    Where my extended soul is fixed;
But Fate does iron wedges drive,
    And always crowds itself betwixt.

For Fate with jealous eye does see
    Two perfect loves, nor lets them close;
Their union would her ruin be,
    And her tyrannic power depose.

And therefore her decrees of steel

    Us as the distant poles have placed,

(Though Love's whole world on us doth wheel),

    Not by themselves to be embraced,


Unless the giddy heaven fall,

    And earth some new convulsion tear.

And, us to join, the world should all

    Be cramp'd into a planisphere.


As lines, so love's oblique, may well

    Themselves in every angle greet:

But ours, so truly parallel,

    Though infinite, can never meet.


Therefore the love which us doth bind,

    But Fate so enviously debars,

Is the conjunction of the mind,

    And opposition of the stars.

## The Picture of little T.C. in a Prospect of Flowers

See with what simplicity
This Nimph begins her golden daies!
In the green Grass she loves to lie,
And there with her fair Aspect tames
The Wilder flow'rs, and gives them names:
But only with the Roses playes;
        And them does tell
What Colour best becomes them, and what Smell.

Who can foretel for what high cause
This Darling of the Gods was born!
Yet this is She whose chaster Laws
The wanton Love shall one day fear,
And, under her command severe,
See his Bow broke and Ensigns torn.
        Happy, who can
Appease this virtuous Enemy of Man!

O then let me in time compound,
And parly with those conquering Eyes;
Ere they have try'd their force to wound,
Ere, with their glancing wheels, they drive
In Triumph over Hearts that strive,
And them that yield but more despise.

Let me be laid,

Where I may see thy Glories from some Shade.


Mean time, whilst every verdant thing

It self does at thy Beauty charm,

Reform the errours of the Spring;

Make that the Tulips may have share

Of sweetness, seeing they are fair;

And Roses of their thorns disarm:

        But most procure

That Violets may a longer Age endure.


But O young beauty of the Woods,

Whom Nature courts with fruits and flow'rs,

Gather the Flow'rs, but spare the Buds;

Lest Flora angry at thy crime,

To kill her Infants in their prime,

Do quickly make th' Example Yours;

        And, ere we see,

Nip in the blossome all our hopes and Thee.

## The Match

Nature had long a Treasure made
Of all her choisest store;
Fearing, when She should be decay'd,
To beg in vain for more.

Her Orientest Colours there,
And Essences most pure,
With sweetest Perfumes hoarded were,
All as she thought secure.

She seldom them unlock'd, or us'd,
But with the nicest care;
For, with one grain of them diffus'd,
She could the World repair.

But likeness soon together drew
What she did separate lay;
Of which one perfect Beauty grew,
And that was Celia.

Love wisely had of long fore-seen
That he must once grow old;
And therefore stor'd a Magazine,
To save him from the cold.

He kept the several Cells repleat
With Nitre thrice refin'd;
The Naphta's and the Sulphurs heat,
And all that burns the Mind.

He fortifi'd the double Gate,
And rarely thither came,
For, with one Spark of these, he streight
All Nature could inflame.

Till, by vicinity so long,
A nearer Way they sought;
And, grown magnetically strong,
Into each other wrought.

Thus all his fewel did unite
To make one fire high:
None ever burn'd so hot, so bright:
And Celia that am I.

So we alone the happy rest,
Whilst all the World is poor,
And have within our Selves possest
All Love's and Nature's store.

# The Mower against Gardens

Luxurious man, to bring his vice in use,
   Did after him the world seduce,
And from the fields the flowers and plants allure,
   Where Nature was most plain and pure.
He first inclosed within the gardens square
   A dead and standing pool of air,
And a more luscious earth for them did knead,
   Which stupefied them while it fed.
The pink grew then as double as his mind;
   The nutriment did change the kind.
With strange perfumes he did the roses taint;
   And flowers themselves were taught to paint.
The tulip white did for complexion seek,
   And learned to interline its cheek;
Its onion root they then so high did hold,
   That one was for a meadow sold:
Another world was searched through oceans new,
   To find the marvel of Peru;
And yet these rarities might be allowed
   To man, that sovereign thing and proud,
Had he not dealt between the bark and tree,
   Forbidden mixtures there to see.
No plant now knew the stock from which it came;
   He grafts upon the wild the tame,

That the uncertain and adulterate fruit

    Might put the palate in dispute.

His green seraglio has its eunuchs too,

    Lest any tyrant him outdo ;

And in the cherry he does Nature vex,

    To procreate without a sex.

'Tis all enforced, the fountain and the grot,

    While the sweet fields do lie forgot,

Where willing Nature does to all dispense

    A wild and fragrant innocence;

And fauns and fairies do the meadows till

    More by their presence than their skill.

Their statues polished by some ancient hand,

    May to adorn the gardens stand;

But, howsoe'er the figures do excel,

    The Gods themselves with us do dwell.

# Damon the Mower

Heark how the Mower Damon Sung,
With love of Juliana stung!
While ev'ry thing did seem to paint
The Scene more fit for his complaint.
Like her fair Eyes the day was fair;
But scorching like his am'rous Care.
Sharp like his Sythe his Sorrow was,
And wither'd like his Hopes the Grass.

Oh what unusual Heats are here,
Which thus our Sun-burn'd Meadows sear!
The Grass-hopper its pipe gives ore;
And hamstring'd Frogs can dance no more.
But in the brook the green Frog wades;
And Grass-hoppers seek out the shades.
Only the Snake, that kept within,
Now glitters in its second skin.

This heat the Sun could never raise,
Nor Dog-star so inflame's the dayes.
It from an higher Beauty grow'th,
Which burns the Fields and Mower both:
Which made the Dog, and makes the Sun
Hotter then his own Phaeton.

Not July causeth these Extremes,
But Juliana's scorching beams.

Tell me where I may pass the Fires
Of the hot day, or hot desires.
To what cool Cave shall I descend,
Or to what gelid Fountain bend?
Alas! I look for Ease in vain,
When Remedies themselves complain.
No moisture but my Tears do rest,
Nor Cold but in her Icy Breast.

How long wilt Thou, fair Shepheardess,
Esteem me, and my Presents less?
To Thee the harmless Snake I bring,
Disarmed of its teeth and sting.
To Thee Chameleons changing-hue,
And Oak leaves tipt with hony-dew.
Yet Thou ungrateful hast not sought
Nor what they are, nor who them brought.

I am the Mower Damon, known
Through all the Meadows I have mown.
On me the Morn her dew distills
Before her darling Daffadils.
And, if at Noon my toil me heat,

The Sun himself licks off my Sweat.

While, going home, the Ev'ning sweet

In cowslip-water bathes my feet.


What, though the piping Shepherd stock

The plains with an unnumber'd Flock,

This Sithe of mine discovers wide

More ground than all his Sheep do hide.

With this the golden fleece I shear

Of all these Closes ev'ry Year.

And though in Wooll more poor than they,

Yet am I richer far in Hay.


Nor am I so deform'd to sight,

If in my Sithe I looked right;

In which I see my Picture done,

As in a crescent Moon the Sun.

The deathless Fairyes take me oft

To lead them in their Danses soft:

And, when I tune myself to sing,

About me they contract their Ring.


How happy might I still have mow'd,

Had not Love here his Thistles sow'd!

But now I all the day complain,

Joyning my Labour to my Pain;

And with my Sythe cut down the Grass,
Yet still my Grief is where it was:
But, when the Iron blunter grows,
Sighing I whet my Sythe and Woes.

While thus he threw his Elbow round,
Depopulating all the Ground,
And, with his whistling Sythe, does cut
Each stroke between the Earth and Root,
The edged Stele by careless chance
Did into his own Ankle glance;
And there among the Grass fell down,
By his own Sythe, the Mower mown.

Alas! said He, these hurts are slight
To those that dye by Love's despight.
With Shepherd's-purse, and Clown's-all-heal,
The Blood I stanch, and Wound I seal.
Only for him no Cure is found,
Whom Juliana's Eyes do wound.
'Tis death alone that this must do:
For Death thou art a Mower too.

# The Mower to the Glo-Worms

Ye living Lamps, by whose dear light
The Nightingale does sit so late,
And studying all the Summer-night,
Her matchless Songs does meditate;

Ye Country Comets, that portend
No War, nor Princes funeral,
Shining unto no higher end
Then to presage the Grasses fall;

Ye Glo-worms, whose officious Flame
To wandring Mowers shows the way,
That in the Night have lost their aim,
And after foolish Fires do stray;

Your courteous Lights in vain you wast,
Since Juliana here is come,
For She my Mind hath so displac'd
That I shall never find my home.

## The Mower's Song

My mind was once the true survey
Of all these meadows fresh and gay,
And in the greenness of the grass
Did see its hopes as in a glass;
When JULIANA came, and she,
What I do to the grass, does to my thoughts and me.


But these, while I with sorrow pine,
Grew more luxuriant still and fine,
That not one blade of grass you spied,
But had a flower on either side;
When JULIANA came, and she,
What I do to the grass, does to my thoughts and me.


Unthankful meadows, could you so
A fellowship so true forego,
And in your gaudy May-games meet,
While I lay trodden under feet?
When JULIANA came, and she,
What I do to the grass, does to my thoughts and me?

But what you in compassion ought,

Shall now by my revenge be wrought;

And flowers, and grass, and I, and all,

Will in one common ruin fall;

For JULIANA comes, and she,

What I do to the grass, does to my thoughts and me.


And thus, ye meadows, which have been

Companions of my thoughts more green,

Shall now the heraldry become

With which I shall adorn my tomb;

For JULIANA came, and she,

What I do to the grass, does to my thoughts and me.

## Ametas and Thestylis making Hay-Ropes

### Ametas

Think'st Thou that this Love can stand,
Whilst Thou still dost say me nay?
Love unpaid does soon disband:
Love binds Love as Hay binds Hay.

### Thestylis

Think'st Thou that this Rope would twine
If we both should turn one way?
Where both parties so combine,
Neither Love will twist nor Hay.

### Ametas

Thus you vain Excuses find,
Which your selve and us delay:
And Love tyes a Woman's Mind
Looser than with Ropes of Hay.

### Thestylis

What you cannot constant hope
Must be taken as you may.

**Ametas**

Then let's both lay by our Rope,

And go kiss within the Hay.

## Musick's Empire

First was the World as one great Cymbal made,
Where Jarring Windes to infant Nature plaid.
All Musick was a solitary sound,
To hollow Rocks and murm'ring Fountains bound.

*Jubal* first made the wilder Notes agree;
And *Jubal* tun'd Musick's *Jubilee:*
He call'd the *Ecchoes* from their sullen Cell,
And built the Organs City where they dwell.

Each sought a consort in that lovely place;
And Virgin Trebles wed the manly Base.
From whence the Progeny of numbers new
Into harmonious Colonies withdrew.

Some to the Lute, some to the Viol went,
And others chose the Cornet eloquent.
These practising the Wind, and those the Wire,
To sing Mens Triumphs, or in Heavens quire.

Then Musick, the Mosaique of the Air,
Did of all these a Solemn noise prepare:
With which She gain'd the Empire of the Ear,
Including all between the Earth and Sphear.

Victorious sounds! yet here your Homage do

Unto a gentler Conqueror than you;

Who though He flies the Musick of his praise,

Would with you Heavens Hallelujahs raise.

# The Garden

How vainly men themselves amaze
To win the palm, the oak, or bays;
And their uncessant labors see
Crowned from some single herb or tree,
Whose short and narrow-vergèd shade
Does prudently their toils upbraid;
While all the flowers and trees do close
To weave the garlands of repose.

Fair Quiet, have I found thee here,
And Innocence, thy sister dear!
Mistaken long, I sought you then
In busy companies of men:
Your sacred plants, if here below,
Only among the plants will grow;
Society is all but rude,
To this delicious solitude.

No white nor red was ever seen
So amorous as this lovely green;
Fond lovers, cruel as their flame,
Cut in these trees their mistress' name.
Little, alas, they know or heed,

How far these beauties hers exceed!
Fair trees! wheresoe'er your barks I wound
No name shall but your own be found.

When we have run our passion's heat,
Love hither makes his best retreat:
The gods who mortal beauty chase,
Still in a tree did end their race.
Apollo hunted Daphne so,
Only that she might laurel grow,
And Pan did after Syrinx speed,
Not as a nymph, but for a reed.

What wondrous life is this I lead!
Ripe apples drop about my head;
The luscious clusters of the vine
Upon my mouth do crush their wine;
The nectarine and curious peach
Into my hands themselves do reach;
Stumbling on melons as I pass,
Insnared with flowers, I fall on grass.

Meanwhile the mind, from pleasure less,
Withdraws into its happiness:
The mind, that ocean where each kind
Does straight its own resemblance find;

Yet it creates, transcending these,

Far other worlds, and other seas;

Annihilating all that's made

To a green thought in a green shade.


Here at the fountain's sliding foot,

Or at some fruit-tree's mossy root,

Casting the body's vest aside,

My soul into the boughs does glide:

There like a bird it sits and sings,

Then whets and combs its silver wings;

And, till prepared for longer flight,

Waves in its plumes the various light.


Such was that happy garden-state,

While man there walked without a mate:

After a place so pure and sweet,

What other help could yet be meet!

But 'twas beyond a mortal's share

To wander solitary there:

Two paradises 'twere in one

To live in Paradise alone.


How well the skillful gard'ner drew

Of flowers and herbs this dial new;

Where from above the milder sun

Does through a fragrant zodiac run;

And, as it works, th' industrious bee

Computes its time as well as we.

How could such sweet and wholesome hours

Be reckoned but with herbs and flowers!

## The Second Chorus from Seneca's Tragedy, Thyestes

*Stet quicunque volet potens*
*Aulae culmine lubrico etc.*

Climb at *Court* for me that will
Tottering Favour's slipp'ry hill.
All I seek is to lye still.
Settled in some secret Nest
In calm Leisure let me rest;
And far off the publick Stage
Pass away my silent Age.
Thus when without noise, unknown,
I have liv'd out all my span,
I shall dye, without a groan,
An old honest Country man.
Who expos'd to others Eyes,
Into his own Heart ne'r pry's,
Death to him's a Strange surprise.

## Horatian Ode upon Cromwell's Return from Ireland

The forward youth that would appear,

Must now forsake his Muses dear,

    Nor in the shadows sing

    His numbers languishing.


'Tis time to leave the books in dust,

And oil the unused armour's rust,

    Removing from the wall

    The corslet of the hall.


So restless Cromwell could not cease

In the inglorious arts of peace,

    But through adventurous war

    Urgèd his active star:


And like the three-fork'd lightning, first

Breaking the clouds where it was nurst,

    Did thorough his own Side

    His fiery way divide:


For 'tis all one to courage high,

The emulous, or enemy;

    And with such, to enclose

Is more than to oppose;

Then burning through the air he went,
And palaces and temples rent;
   And Cæsar's head at last
   Did through his laurels blast.

'Tis madness to resist or blame
The face of angry heaven's flame;
   And if we would speak true,
   Much to the Man is due

Who, from his private gardens, where
He lived reservèd and austere,
   (As if his highest plot
   To plant the bergamot),

Could by industrious valour climb
To ruin the great work of time,
   And cast the Kingdoms old
   Into another mould;

Though Justice against Fate complain,
And plead the ancient Rights in vain—
   But those do hold or break
   As men are strong or weak;

Nature, that hateth emptiness,

Allows of penetration less,

    And therefore must make room

    Where greater spirits come.


What field of all the civil war

Where his were not the deepest scar?

    And Hampton shows what part

    He had of wiser art,


Where, twining subtle fears with hope,

He wove a net of such a scope

    That Charles himself might chase

    To Carisbrook's narrow case,


That thence the Royal actor borne

The tragic scaffold might adorn:

    While round the armèd bands

    Did clap their bloody hands.


He nothing common did or mean

Upon that memorable scene,

    But with his keener eye

    The axe's edge did try;

Nor call'd the Gods, with vulgar spite,

To vindicate his helpless right;

   But bow'd his comely head

   Down, as upon a bed.


—This was that memorable hour

Which first assured the forcèd power:

   So when they did design

   The Capitol's first line,


A Bleeding Head, where they begun,

Did fright the architects to run;

   And yet in that the State

   Foresaw its happy fate!


And now the Irish are ashamed

To see themselves in one year tamed:

   So much one man can do

   That does both act and know.


They can affirm his praises best,

And have, though overcome, confest

   How good he is, how just

   And fit for highest trust.


Nor yet grown stiffer with command,

But still in the Republic's hand—
    How fit he is to sway
    That can so well obey!

He to the Commons' feet presents
A Kingdom for his first year's rents,
    And (what he may) forbears
    His fame, to make it theirs:

And has his sword and spoils ungirt
To lay them at the Public's skirt;
    So when the falcon high
    Falls heavy from the sky,

She, having kill'd, no more doth search
But on the next green bough to perch,
    Where, when he first does lure
    The falconer has her sure.

—What may not then our Isle presume
While victory his crest does plume?
    What may not others fear
    If thus he crowns each year?

As Cæsar he, ere long, to Gaul,
To Italy an Hannibal,

And to all States not free

Shall climacteric be.


The Pict no shelter now shall find

Within his parti-colour'd mind,

But from this valour sad

Shrink underneath the plaid—


Happy, if in the tufted brake

The English hunter him mistake,

Nor lay his hounds in near

The Caledonian deer.


But Thou, the War's and Fortune's son,

March indefatigably on;

And for the last effect

Still keep the sword erect:


Besides the force it has to fright

The spirits of the shady night,

The same arts that did gain

A power, must it maintain.

## Upon the Hill and Grove at Billborow
## To the Lord Fairfax

See how the archèd earth does here
Rise in a perfect hemisphere !
The stiffest compass could not strike
A line more circular and like,
Nor softest pencil draw a brow
So equal as this hill does bow ;
It seems as for a model laid,
And that the world by it was made.
Here learn, ye mountains more unjust,
Which to abrupter greatness thrust,
That do, with your hook-shouldered height,
The earth deform, and heaven fright,
For whose excrescence, ill designed,
Nature must a new centre find,
Learn here those humble steps to tread,
Which to securer glory lead.
See what a soft access, and wide,
Lies open to its grassy side,
Nor with the rugged path deters
The feet of breathless travellers ;
See then how courteous it ascends,
And all the way it rises, bends,

Nor for itself the height does gain,

But only strives to raise the plain ;

Yet thus it all the field commands,

And in unenvied greatness stands,

Discerning further than the cliff

Of heaven-daring Teneriff.

How glad the weary seamen haste,

When they salute it from the mast !

By night, the northern star their way

Directs, and this no less by day.

Upon its crest, this mountain grave,

A plume of agèd trees does wave.

No hostile hand durst e'er invade,

With impious steel, the sacred shade ;

For something always did appear

Of the GREAT MASTER'S terror there,

And men could hear his armour still,

Rattling through all the grove and hill.

Fear of the MASTER, and respect

Of the great nymph, did it protect ;

VERA, the nymph, that him inspired,

To whom he often here retired,

And on these oaks ingraved her name,

Such wounds alone these woods became ;

But ere he well the barks could part,

'Twas writ already in their heart ;

For they, 'tis credible, have sense,

As we, of love and reverence,

And underneath the coarser rind

The genius of the house do bind.

Hence they successes seem to know,

And in their Lord's advancement grow ;

But in no memory were seen,

As under this, so straight and green ;

Yet now no farther strive to shoot,

Contented, if they fix their root,

Nor to the wind's uncertain gust

Their prudent heads too far entrust.

Only sometimes a fluttering breeze

Discourses with the breathing trees,

Which in their modest whispers name

Those acts that swelled the cheeks of Fame.

" Much other groves," say they, "than these,

And other hills, him once did please.

Through groves of pikes he thundered then,

And mountains raised of dying men.

For all the civic garlands due

To him, our branches are but few;

Nor are our trunks enough to bear

The trophies of one fertile year."

'Tis true, ye trees, nor ever spoke

More certain oracles in oak ;

But peace, if you his favour prize!

That courage its own praises flies:

Therefore to your obscurer seats

From his own brightness he retreats ;

Nor he the hills, without the groves,

Nor height, but with retirement, loves.

# Upon Appleton House, to my Lord Fairfax

I

Within this sober Frame expect

Work of no Forrain Architect;

That unto Caves the Quarries drew,

And Forrests did to Pastures hew;

Who of his great Design in pain

Did for a Model vault his Brain,

Whose Columnes should so high be rais'd

To arch the Brows that on them gaz'd.


II

Why should of all things Man unrul'd

Such unproportion'd dwellings build?

The Beasts are by their Denns exprest:

And Birds contrive an equal Nest;

The low roof'd Tortoises do dwell

In cases fit of Tortoise-shell:

No Creature loves an empty space;

Their Bodies measure out their Place.


III

But He, superfluously spread,

Demands more room alive then dead.

And in his hollow Palace goes

Where Winds as he themselves may lose.
What need of all this Marble Crust
T'impark the wanton Mose of Dust,
That thinks by Breadth the World t'unite
Though the first Builders fail'd in Height?

IV

But all things are composed here
Like Nature, orderly and near:
In which we the Dimensions find
Of that more sober Age and Mind,
When larger sized Men did stoop
To enter at a narrow loop;
As practising, in doors so strait,
To strain themselves through Heaven's Gate.

V

And surely when the after Age
Shall hither come in Pilgrimage,
These sacred Places to adore,
By Vere and Fairfax trod before,
Men will dispute how their Extent
Within such dwarfish Confines went:
And some will smile at this, as well
As Romulus his Bee-like Cell.

## VI

Humility alone designs

Those short but admirable Lines,

By which, ungirt and unconstrain'd,

Things greater are in less contain'd.

Let others vainly strive t'immure

The Circle in the Quadrature!

These holy Mathematicks can

In ev'ry Figure equal Man.

## VII

Yet thus the laden House does sweat,

And scarce indures the Master great:

But where he comes the swelling Hall

Stirs, and the Square grows Spherical;

More by his Magnitude distrest,

Than he is by its straitness prest:

And too officiously it slights

That in it self which him delights.

## VIII

So Honour better Lowness bears,

Then That unwonted Greatness wears

Height with a certain Grace does bend,

But low Things clownishly ascend.

And yet what needs there here Excuse,

Where ev'ry Thing does answer Use?
Where neatness nothing can condemn,
Nor Pride invent what to contemn?

## IX

A Stately Frontispice Of Poor
Adorns without the open Door:
Nor less the Rooms within commends
Daily new Furniture Of Friends.
The House was built upon the Place
Only as for a Mark Of Grace;
And for an Inn to entertain
Its Lord a while, but not remain.

## X

Him Bishops-Hill, or Denton may,
Or Bilbrough, better hold than they:
But Nature here hath been so free
As if she said leave this to me.
Art would more neatly have defac'd
What she had laid so sweetly wast;
In fragrant Gardens, shaddy Woods,
Deep Meadows, and transparent Floods.

## XI

While with slow Eyes we these survey,

And on each pleasant footstep stay,

We opportunly may relate

The progress of this Houses Fate.

A Nunnery first gave it birth.

For Virgin Buildings oft brought forth.

And all that Neighbour-Ruine shows

The Quarries whence this dwelling rose.


XII

Near to this gloomy Cloysters Gates

There dwelt the blooming Virgin Thwates,

Fair beyond Measure, and an Heir

Which might Deformity make fair.

And oft She spent the Summer Suns

Discoursing with the Suttle Nunns.

Whence in these Words one to her weav'd,

(As 'twere by Chance) Thoughts long conceiv'd.


XII

"Within this holy leisure we

Live innocently as you see.

these Walls restrain the World without,

But hedge our Liberty about.

These Bars inclose the wider Den

Of those wild Creatures, called Men.

The Cloyster outward shuts its Gates,

And, from us, locks on them the Grates.

XIV

"Here we, in shining Armour white,

Like Virgin-Amazons do fight.

And our chast Lamps we hourly trim,

Lest the great Bridegroom find them dim.

Our Orient Breaths perfumed are

With insense of incessant Pray'r.

And Holy-water of our Tears

Most strangly our Complexion clears.

XV

"Not Tears of Grief; but such as those

With which calm Pleasure overflows;

Or Pity, when we look on you

That live without this happy Vow.

How should we grieve that must be seen

Each one a Spouse, and each a Queen;

And can in Heaven hence behold

Our brighter Robes and Crowns of Gold?

XVI

"When we have prayed all our Beads,

Some One the holy Legend reads;

While all the rest with Needles paint

The Face and Graces of the Saint.

But what the Linnen can't receive

They in their Lives do interweave.

This Work the Saints best represents;

That serves for Altar's Ornaments.


XVII

"But much it to our work would add

If here your hand, your Face we had:

By it we would our Lady touch;

Yet thus She you resembles much.

Some of your Features, as we sow'd,

Through ev'ry Shrine should be bestow'd.

And in one Beauty we would take

Enough a thousand Saints to make.


XVIII

"And (for I dare not quench the Fire

That me does for your good inspire)

'Twere Sacriledge a Man t'admit

To holy things, for Heaven fit.

I see the Angels in a Crown

On you the Lillies show'ring down:

And round about your Glory breaks,

That something more than humane speaks.

## XIX

"All Beauty, when at such a height,
Is so already consecrate.
Fairfax I know; and long ere this
Have mark'd the Youth, and what he is.
But can he such a Rival seem
For whom you Heav'n should disesteem?
Ah, no! and 'twould more Honour prove
He your Devoto were, than Love.

## XX

"Here live beloved, and obey'd:
Each one your Sister, each your Maid.
And, if our Rule seem strictly pend,
The Rule it self to you shall bend.
Our Abbess too, now far in Age,
Doth your succession near presage.
How soft the yoke on us would lye,
Might such fair Hands as yours it tye!

## XXI

"Your voice, the sweetest of the Quire,
Shall draw Heav'n nearer, raise us higher.
And your Example, if our Head,
Will soon us to perfection lead.
Those Virtues to us all so dear,

Will straight grow Sanctity when here:

And that, once sprung, increase so fast

Till Miracles it work at last.


XXII

"Nor is our Order yet so nice,

Delight to banish as a Vice.

Here Pleasure Piety doth meet;

One perfecting the other Sweet.

So through the mortal fruit we boyl

The Sugars uncorrupting Oyl:

And that which perisht while we pull,

Is thus preserved clear and full.


XXIII

"For such indeed are all our Arts;

Still handling Natures finest Parts.

Flow'rs dress the Altars; for the Clothes,

The Sea-born Amber we compose;

Balms for the griv'd we draw; and pasts

We mold, as Baits for curious tasts.

What need is here of Man? unless

These as sweet Sins we should confess.


XXIV

"Each Night among us to your side

Appoint a fresh and Virgin Bride;

Whom if Our Lord at midnight find,

Yet Neither should be left behind.

Where you may lye as chast in Bed,

As Pearls together billeted.

All Night embracing Arm in Arm,

Like Chrystal pure with Cotton warm.


XXV

"But what is this to all the store

Of Joys you see, and may make more!

Try but a while, if you be wise:

The Tryal neither Costs, nor Tyes."

Now Fairfax seek her promis'd faith:

Religion that dispensed hath;

Which She hence forward does begin;

The Nuns smooth Tongue has suckt her in.


XXVI

Oft, though he knew it was in vain,

Yet would he valiantly complain.

"Is this that Sanctity so great,

An Art by which you finly'r cheat

Hypocrite Witches, hence avant,

Who though in prison yet inchant!

Death only can such Theeves make fast,

As rob though in the Dungeon cast.

## XXVII

"Were there but, when this House was made,

One Stone that a just Hand had laid,

It must have fall'n upon her Head

Who first Thee from thy Faith misled.

And yet, how well soever ment,

With them 'twould soon grow fraudulent

For like themselves they alter all,

And vice infects the very Wall.

## XXVIII

"But sure those Buildings last not long,

Founded by Folly, kept by Wrong.

I know what Fruit their Gardens yield,

When they it think by Night conceal'd.

Fly from their Vices. 'Tis thy 'state,

Not Thee, that they would consecrate.

Fly from their Ruine. How I fear

Though guiltless lest thou perish there."

## XXIX

What should he do? He would respect

Religion, but not Right neglect:

For first Religion taught him Right,

And dazled not but clear'd his sight.

Sometimes resolv'd his Sword he draws,

But reverenceth then the Laws:

For Justice still that Courage led;

First from a Judge, then Souldier bred.


## XXX

Small Honour would be in the Storm.

The Court him grants the lawful Form;

Which licens'd either Peace or Force,

To hinder the unjust Divorce.

Yet still the Nuns his Right debar'd,

Standing upon their holy Guard.

Ill-counsell'd Women, do you know

Whom you resist, or what you do?


## XXXI

Is not this he whose Offspring fierce

Shall fight through all the Universe;

And with successive Valour try

France, Poland, either Germany;

Till one, as long since prophecy'd,

His Horse through conquer'd Britain ride?

Yet, against Fate, his Spouse they kept;

And the great Race would intercept.

## XXXII

Some to the Breach against their Foes
Their Wooden Saints in vain oppose
Another bolder stands at push
With their old Holy-Water Brush.
While the disjointed Abbess threads
The gingling Chain-shot of her Beads.
But their lowd'st Cannon were their Lungs;
And sharpest Weapons were their Tongues.

## XXXIII

But, waving these aside like Flyes,
Young Fairfax through the Wall does rise.
Then th' unfrequented Vault appear'd,
And superstitions vainly fear'd.
The Relicks false were set to view;
Only the Jewels there were true.
But truly bright and holy Thwaites
That weeping at the Altar waites.

## XXXIV

But the glad Youth away her bears,
And to the Nuns bequeaths her Tears:
Who guiltily their Prize bemoan,
Like Gipsies that a Child hath stoln.
Thenceforth (as when th' Inchantment ends

The Castle vanishes or rends)

The wasting Cloister with the rest

Was in one instant dispossest.


XXXV

At the demolishing, this Seat

To Fairfax fell as by Escheat.

And what both Nuns and Founders will'd

'Tis likely better thus fulfill'd,

For if the Virgin prov'd not theirs,

The Cloyster yet remained hers.

Though many a Nun there made her vow,

'Twas no Religious-House till now.


XXXVI

From that blest Bed the Heroe came,

Whom France and Poland yet does fame:

Who, when retired here to Peace,

His warlike Studies could not cease;

But laid these Gardens out in sport

In the just Figure of a Fort;

And with five Bastions it did fence,

As aiming one for ev'ry Sense.


XXXVII

When in the East the Morning Ray

Hangs out the Colours of the Day,

The Bee through these known Allies hums,

Beating the Dian with its Drumms.

Then Flow'rs their drowsie Eylids raise,

Their Silken Ensigns each displayes,

And dries its Pan yet dank with Dew,

And fills its Flask with Odours new.


XXXVIII

These, as their Governour goes by,

In fragrant Vollyes they let fly;

And to salute their Governess

Again as great a charge they press:

None for the Virgin Nymph; for She

Seems with the Flow'rs a Flow'r to be.

And think so still! though not compare

With Breath so sweet, or Cheek so faire.


XXXIX

Well shot ye Firemen! Oh how sweet,

And round your equal Fires do meet;

Whose shrill report no Ear can tell,

But Ecchoes to the Eye and smell.

See how the Flow'rs, as at Parade,

Under their Colours stand displaid:

Each Regiment in order grows,

That of the Tulip, Pinke, and Rose.

XL

But when the vigilant Patroul
Of Stars walks round about the Pole,
Their Leaves, that to the stalks are curl'd,
Seem to their Staves the Ensigns furl'd.
Then in some Flow'rs beloved Hut
Each Bee as Sentinel is shut;
And sleeps so too: but, if once stir'd,
She runs you through, nor askes the Word.

XLI

Oh Thou, that dear and happy Isle
The Garden of the World ere while,
Thou Paradise of four Seas,
Which Heaven planted us to please,
But, to exclude the World, did guard
With watry if not flaming Sword;
What luckless Apple did we tast,
To make us Mortal, and Thee Waste.

XLII

Unhappy! shall we never more
That sweet Militia restore,
When Gardens only had their Towrs,

And all the Garrisons were Flowrs,

When Roses only Arms might bear,

And Men did rosie Garlands wear?

Tulips, in several Colours barr'd,

Were then the Switzers of our Guard.


XLIII

The Gardiner had the Souldier's place,

And his more gentle Forts did trace.

The Nursery of all things green

Was then the only Magazeen.

The Winter Quarters were the Stoves,

Where he the tender Plants removes.

But War all this doth overgrow:

We Ord'nance Plant and Powder sow.


XLIV

And yet their walks one on the Sod

Who, had it pleased him and God,

Might once have made our Gardens spring

Fresh as his own and flourishing.

But he preferr'd to the Cinque Ports

These five imaginary Forts:

And, in those half-dry Trenches, spann'd

Pow'r which the Ocean might command.

## XLV

For he did, with his utmost Skill,

Ambition weed, but Conscience till.

Conscience, that Heaven-nursed Plant,

Which most our Earthly Gardens want.

A prickling leaf it bears, and such

As that which shrinks at ev'ry touch;

But Flow'rs eternal, and divine,

That in the Crowns of Saints do shine.


## XLVI

The sight does from these Bastions ply,

Th' invisible Artilery;

And at proud Cawood-Castle seems

To point the Battery of its Beams.

As if it quarrell'd in the Seat

Th' Ambition of its Prelate great.

But ore the Meads below it plays,

Or innocently seems to gaze.


## XLVII

And now to the Abbyss I pass

Of that unfathomable Grass,

Where Men like Grashoppers appear,

But Grashoppers are Gyants there:

They, in there squeking Laugh, contemn

Us as we walk more low then them:
And, from the Precipices tall
Of the green spir's, to us do call.


XLVIII

To see Men through this Meadow Dive,
We wonder how they rise alive.
As, under Water, none does know
Whether he fall through it or go.
But, as the Marriners that sound,
And show upon their Lead the Ground,
They bring up Flow'rs so to be seen,
And prove they've at the Bottom been.


XLIX

No Scene that turns with Engines strange
Does oftner then these Meadows change,
For when the Sun the Grass hath vext,
The tawny Mowers enter next;
Who seem like Israelites to be,
Walking on foot through a green Sea.
To them the Grassy Deeps divide,
And crowd a Lane to either Side.

L

With whistling Sithe, and Elbow strong,

These Massacre the Grass along:

While one, unknowing, carves the Rail,

Whose yet unfeather'd Quils her fail.

The Edge all bloody from its Breast

He draws, and does his stroke detest;

Fearing the Flesh untimely mow'd

To him a Fate as black forebode.


LI

But bloody Thestylis, that waites

To bring the mowing Camp their Cates,

Greedy as Kites has trust it up,

And forthwith means on it to sup:

When on another quick She lights,

And cryes, he call'd us Israelites;

But now, to make his saying true,

Rails rain for Quails, for Manna Dew.


LII

Unhappy Birds! what does it boot

To build below the Grasses Root;

When Lowness is unsafe as Hight,

And Chance o'retakes what scapeth spight?

And now your Orphan Parents Call

Sounds your untimely Funeral.
Death-Trumpets creak in such a Note,
And 'tis the Sourdine in their Throat.

LIII

Or sooner hatch or higher build:
The Mower now commands the Field;
In whose new Traverse seemeth wrought
A Camp of Battail newly fought:
Where, as the Meads with Hay, the Plain
Lyes quilted ore with Bodies slain:
The Women that with forks it filing,
Do represent the Pillaging.

LIV

And now the careless Victors play,
Dancing the Triumphs of the Hay;
Where every Mowers wholesome Heat
Smells like an Alexanders Sweat.
Their Females fragrant as the Mead
Which they in Fairy Circles tread:
When at their Dances End they kiss,
Their new-made Hay not sweeter is.

## LV

When after this 'tis pil'd in Cocks,
Like a calm Sea it shews the Rocks:
We wondring in the River near
How Boats among them safely steer.
Or, like the Desert Memphis Sand,
Short Pyramids of Hay do stand.
And such the Roman Camps do rise
In Hills for Soldiers' Obsequies.

## LVI

This Scene again withdrawing brings
A new and empty Face of things;
A levell'd space, as smooth and plain,
As Clothes for Lilly strecht to stain.
The World when first created sure
Was such a Table rase and pure.
Or rather such is the Toril
Ere the Bulls enter at Madril.

## LVII

For to this naked equal Flat,
Which Levellers take Pattern at,
The Villagers in common chase
Their Cattle, which it closer rase;
And what below the Sith increast

Is pincht yet nearer by the Breast.

Such, in the painted World, appear'd

Davenant with th'Universal Heard.


LVIII

They seem within the polisht Grass

A landskip drawen in Looking-Glass.

And shrunk in the huge Pasture show

As spots, so shap'd, on Faces do.

Such Fleas, ere they approach the Eye,

In Multiplyiug Glasses lye.

They feed so wide, so slowly move,

As Constellations do above.


LIX

Then, to conclude these pleasant Acts,

Denton sets ope its Cataracts;

And makes the Meadow truly be

(What it but seem'd before) a Sea.

For, jealous of its Lords long stay,

It try's t'invite him thus away.

The River in it self is drown'd,

And Isl's th' astonish Cattle round.


LX

Let others tell the Paradox,

How Eels now bellow in the Ox;

How Horses at their Tails do kick,

Turn'd as they hang to Leeches quick;

How Boats can over Bridges sail;

And Fishes do the Stables scale.

How Salmons trespassing are found;

And Pikes are taken in the Pound.


LXI

But I, retiring from the Flood,

Take Sanctuary in the Wood;

And, while it lasts, my self imbark

In this yet green, yet growing Ark;

Where the first Carpenter might best

Fit Timber for his Keel have Prest.

And where all Creatures might have shares,

Although in Armies, not in Paires.


LXII

The double Wood of ancient Stocks

Link'd in so thick, an Union locks,

It like two Pedigrees appears,

On one hand Fairfax, th' other Veres:

Of whom though many fell in War,

Yet more to Heaven shooting are:

And, as they Natures Cradle deckt,

Will in green Age her Hearse expect.

## LXIII

When first the Eye this Forrest sees
It seems indeed as Wood not Trees:
As if their Neighbourhood so old
To one great Trunk them all did mold.
There the huge Bulk takes place, as ment
To thrust up a Fifth Element;
And stretches still so closely wedg'd
As if the Night within were hedg'd.

## LXIV

Dark all without it knits; within
It opens passable and thin;
And in as loose an order grows,
As the Corinthean Porticoes.
The Arching Boughs unite between
The Columnes of the Temple green;
And underneath the winged Quires
Echo about their tuned Fires.

## LXV

The Nightingale does here make choice
To sing the Tryals of her Voice.
Low Shrubs she sits in, and adorns
With Musick high the squatted Thorns.

But highest Oakes stoop down to hear,
And listning Elders prick the Ear.
The Thorn, lest it should hurt her, draws
Within the Skin its shrunken claws.

## LXVI

But I have for my Musick found
A Sadder, yet more pleasing Sound:
The Stock-doves whose fair necks are grac'd
With Nuptial Rings their Ensigns chast;
Yet always, for some Cause unknown,
Sad pair unto the Elms they moan.
O why should such a Couple mourn,
That in so equal Flames do burn!

## LXVII

Then as I carless on the Bed
Of gelid Straw-berryes do tread,
And through the Hazles thick espy
The hatching Thrastle's shining Eye,
The Heron from the Ashes top,
The eldest of its young lets drop,
As if it Stork-like did pretend
That Tribute to its Lord to send.

## LXVIII

But most the Hewel's wonders are,

Who here has the Holt-felsters care.

He walks still upright from the Root,

Meas'ring the Timber with his Foot;

And all the way, to keep it clean,

Doth from the Bark the Wood-moths glean.

He, with his Beak, examines well

Which fit to stand and which to fell.


## LXIX

The good he numbers up, and hacks;

As if he mark'd them with the Ax.

But where he, tinkling with his Beak,

Does find the hollow Oak to speak,

That for his building he designs,

And through the tainted Side he mines.

Who could have thought the tallest Oak

Should fall by such a feeble Stroke!


## LXX

Nor would it, had the Tree not fed

A Traitor-worm, within it bred.

(As first our Flesh corrupt within

Tempts impotent and bashful Sin.)

And yet that Worm triumphs not long,

But serves to feed the Hewels young.
While the Oake seems to fall content,
Viewing the Treason's Punishment.

## LXXI

Thus I, easie Philosopher,
Among the Birds and Trees confer:
And little now to make me, wants
Or of the Fowles, or of the Plants.
Give me but Wings as they, and I
Streight floting on the Air shall fly:
Or turn me but, and you shall see
I was but an inverted Tree.

## LXXII

Already I begin to call
In their most-learned Original:
And where I Language want, my Signs
The Bird upon the Bough divines;
And more attentive there doth sit
Then if She were with Lime-twigs knit.
No Leaf does tremble in the Wind
Which I returning cannot find.

## LXXIII

Out of these scatter'd Sibyls Leaves

Strange Prophecies my Phancy weaves:

And in one History consumes,

Like Mexique-Paintings, all the Plumes.

What Rome, Greece, Palestine, ere said

I in this light Mosaick read.

Thrice happy he who, not mistook,

Hath read in Natures mystick Book.


## LXXIV

And see how Chance's better Wit

Could with a Mask my studies hit!

The Oak-Leaves me embroyder all,

Between which Caterpillars crawl:

And Ivy, with familiar trails,

Me licks, and clasps, and curles, and hales.

Under this antick Cope I move

Like some great Prelate of the Grove,


## LXXV

Then, languishing with ease, I toss

On Pallets swoln of Velvet Moss;

While the Wind, cooling through the Boughs,

Flatters with Air my panting Brows.

Thanks for my Rest ye Mossy Banks,

And unto you cool Zephyr's Thanks,

Who, as my Hair, my Thoughts too shed,

And winnow from the Chaff my Head.


LXXVI

How safe, methinks, and strong, behind

These Trees have I incamp'd my Mind;

Where Beauty, aiming at the Heart,

Bends in some Tree its useless Dart;

And where the World no certain Shot

Can make, or me it toucheth not.

But I on it securely play,

And gaul its Horsemen all the Day.


LXXVII

Bind me ye Woodbines in your 'twines,

Curle me about ye gadding Vines,

And Oh so close your Circles lace,

That I may never leave this Place:

But, lest your Fetters prove too weak,

Ere I your Silken Bondage break,

Do you, O Brambles, chain me too,

And courteous Briars nail me though.

## LXXVIII

Here in the Morning tye my Chain,

Where the two Woods have made a Lane;

While, like a Guard on either side,

The Trees before their Lord divide;

This, like a long and equal Thread,

Betwixt two Labyrinths does lead.

But, where the Floods did lately drown,

There at the Ev'ning stake me down.


## LXXIX

For now the Waves are fal'n and dry'd,

And now the Meadows fresher dy'd;

Whose Grass, with moister colour dasht,

Seems as green Silks but newly washt.

No Serpent new nor Crocodile

Remains behind our little Nile;

Unless it self you will mistake,

Among these Meads the only Snake.


## LXXX

See in what wanton harmless folds

It ev'ry where the Meadow holds;

And its yet muddy back doth lick,

Till as a Chrystal Mirrour slick;

Where all things gaze themselves, and doubt

If they be in it or without.

And for his shade which therein shines,

Narcissus like, the Sun too pines.


LXXXI

Oh what a Pleasure 'tis to hedge

My Temples here with heavy sedge;

Abandoning my lazy Side,

Stretcht as a Bank unto the Tide;

Or to suspend my sliding Foot

On the Osiers undermined Root,

And in its Branches tough to hang,

While at my Lines the Fishes twang!


LXXXII

But now away my Hooks, my Quills,

And Angles, idle Utensils.

The young Maria walks to night:

Hide trifling Youth thy Pleasures slight.

'Twere shame that such judicious Eyes

Should with such Toyes a Man surprize;

She that already is the Law

Of all her Sex, her Ages Aw.

## LXXXIII

See how loose Nature, in respect

To her, it self doth recollect;

And every thing so whisht and fine,

Starts forth with to its Bonne Mine.

The Sun himself, of Her aware,

Seems to descend with greater Care,

And lest She see him go to Bed,

In blushing Clouds conceales his Head.


## LXXXIV

So when the Shadows laid asleep

From underneath these Banks do creep,

And on the River as it flows

With Eben Shuts begin to close;

The modest Halcyon comes in sight,

Flying betwixt the Day and Night;

And such an horror calm and dumb,

Admiring Nature does benum.


## LXXXV

The viscous Air, wheres'ere She fly,

Follows and sucks her Azure dy;

The gellying Stream compacts below,

If it might fix her shadow so;

The Stupid Fishes hang, as plain

As Flies in Chrystal overt'ane,

And Men the silent Scene assist,

Charm'd with the saphir-winged Mist.


LXXXVI

Maria such, and so doth hush

The World, and through the Ev'ning rush.

No new-born Comet such a Train

Draws through the Skie, nor Star new-slain.

For streight those giddy Rockets fail,

Which from the putrid Earth exhale,

But by her Flames, in Heaven try'd,

Nature is wholly vitrifi'd.


LXXXVII

'Tis She that to these Gardens gave

That wondrous Beauty which they have;

She streightness on the Woods bestows;

To Her the Meadow sweetness owes;

Nothing could make the River be

So Chrystal-pure but only She;

She yet more Pure, Sweet, Streight, and Fair,

Then Gardens, Woods, Meads, Rivers are.

## LXXXVIII

Therefore what first She on them spent,

They gratefully again present.

The Meadow Carpets where to tread;

The Garden Flow'rs to Crown Her Head;

And for a Glass the limpid Brook,

Where She may all her Beautyes look;

But, since She would not have them seen,

The Wood about her draws a Skreen.


## LXXXIX

For She, to higher Beauties rais'd,

Disdains to be for lesser prais'd.

She counts her Beauty to converse

In all the Languages as hers;

Not yet in those her self imployes

But for the Wisdome, not the Noyse;

Nor yet that Wisdome would affect,

But as 'tis Heavens Dialect.


## XC

Blest Nymph! that couldst so soon prevent

Those Trains by Youth against thee meant;

Tears (watry Shot that pierce the Mind;)

And Sighs (Loves Cannon charg'd with Wind;)

True Praise (That breaks through all defence;)

And feign'd complying Innocence;

But knowing where this Ambush lay,

She scap'd the safe, but roughest Way.


XCI

This 'tis to have been from the first

In a Domestick Heaven nurst,

Under the Discipline severe

Of Fairfax, and the starry Vere;

Where not one object can come nigh

But pure, and spotless as the Eye;

And Goodness doth it self intail

On Females, if there want a Male.


XCII

Go now fond Sex that on your Face

Do all your useless Study place,

Nor once at Vice your Brows dare knit

Lest the smooth Forehead wrinkled sit

Yet your own Face shall at you grin,

Thorough the Black-bag of your Skin;

When knowledge only could have fill'd

And Virtue all those Furows till'd.

XCIII

Hence She with Graces more divine

Supplies beyond her Sex the Line;

And, like a sprig of Misleto,

On the Fairfacian Oak does grow;

Whence, for some universal good,

The Priest shall cut the sacred Bud;

While her glad Parents most rejoice,

And make their Destiny their Choice.


XCIV

Mean time ye Fields, Springs, Bushes, Flow'rs,

Where yet She leads her studious Hours,

(Till Fate her worthily translates,

And find a Fairfax for our Thwaites)

Employ the means you have by Her,

And in your kind your selves preferr;

That, as all Virgins She preceds,

So you all Woods, Streams, Gardens, Meads.


XCV

For you Thessalian Tempe's Seat

Shall now be scorn'd as obsolete;

Aranjuez, as less, disdain'd;

The Bel-Retiro as constrain'd;

But name not the Idalian Grove,

For 'twas the Seat of wanton Love;

Much less the Deads' Elysian Fields,

Yet nor to them your Beauty yields.


XCVI

'Tis not, what once it was, the World;

But a rude heap together hurl'd;

All negligently overthrown,

Gulfes, Deserts, Precipices, Stone.

Your lesser World contains the same.

But in more decent Order tame;

You Heaven's Center, Nature's Lap.

And Paradice's only Map.


XCVII

But now the Salmon-Fishers moist

Their Leathern Boats begin to hoist;

And, like Antipodes in Shoes,

Have shod their Heads in their Canoos.

How Tortoise like, but not so slow,

These rational Amphibii go?

Let's in: for the dark Hemisphere

Does now like one of them appear.

Printed in Great Britain
by Amazon